OUR PLACE IN GOD THROUGH

POSITION, PURPOSE, PROMISE, POWER, PROTECTION, PROSPERITY, PEACE, PERFECTION, PROVISION, PRIZE

Alisa Hope Wagner

Marked Writers Publishing

OUR PLACE IN GOD THROUGH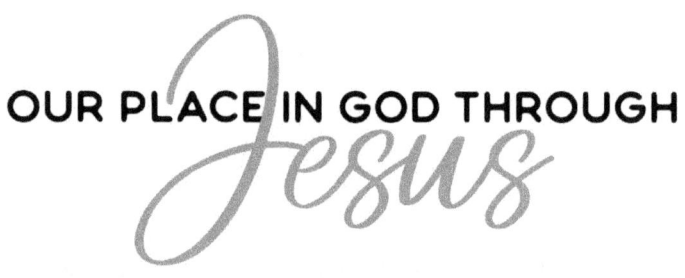

POSITION, PURPOSE, PROMISE, POWER, PROTECTION, PROSPERITY, PEACE, PERFECTION, PROVISION, PRIZE

Copyright @ 2023 by Alisa Hope Wagner
All rights reserved
Marked Writers Publishing
www.alisahopewagner.com

Scriptures taken from various translations of the Bible found at www.biblegateway.com.

Cover designed by Holly Smith
Author Photo by Lori Stead at
https://www.wetsilver.com/

ISBN: 978-1-963190-04-5

OUR PLACE IN GOD THROUGH *Jesus*

POSITION, PURPOSE, PROMISE, POWER,
PROTECTION, PROSPERITY, PEACE,
PERFECTION, PROVISION, PRIZE

DEDICATION

Daniel – the man of my dreams

Isaac Jeremiah – my prophet

Levi Daniel – my shepherd

Karis Ruth – my graceful companion

Editing Team – Holly Smith and Patricia Coughlin

Holy Spirit – my writing partner

INTRODUCTION

"But [we are different, because] **our citizenship is in heaven**. And from there we eagerly await [the coming of] the Savior, the Lord Jesus Christ" (Philippians 3.20 AMP).

Because of the Finished Work of Jesus Christ on the Cross, we now have a **Place in God**, our Creator. This space we occupy in God's presence entails ten supernatural realities: **Position, Purpose, Promise, Power, Protection, Prosperity, Peace, Perfection, Provision and Prize**—all attributes of our Heavenly Father's goodness.

The Bible says that if we have accepted Jesus as our Lord and Savior, we are reconciled (restored to friendly relations) back to God (Romans 5:10-11). This restoration is a gift that we can never earn. God so loves us that He initiated the Gift of Salvation through Jesus while we were yet undeserving (Romans 5.8). All we must do is see our need for this gift and accept it by confessing and believing. *Simple.*

"That if you **confess** with your mouth the Lord Jesus and **believe** in your heart that God has raised Him from the dead, you will be saved" (Romans 10.9 NKJV).

Once we accept the Gift of Salvation, we now have a **Place in God**, and again this space includes but is not limited to **Position, Purpose, Promise, Power, Protection, Prosperity, Peace, Perfection, Provision and Prize.**

Gift of Salvation

If you would like the Gift of Salvation and find your true identity in Christ and find your Place in God, all you have to do is pray the simple prayer below and believe in your heart that Jesus died to be your Lord and Savior.

"Jesus, I believe You died to reconcile me back to my Creator God. Thank You for paying the debt of my sin with Your Precious Blood. I ask You to come into my heart and life and save me from darkness, sin and shame. I declare that I am a new person in Christ, and I can now have a growing relationship with my Heavenly Father. Now I ask that God's Spirit, the Holy Spirit, pour over me with a mighty flood of His

Presence, so I can be Placed directly in the will, favor and blessings of God. I ask this in Jesus' name, Amen."

TABLE OF CONTENTS

POSITION	1
PURPOSE	6
PROMISE	11
POWER	17
PROTECTION	23
PROSPERITY	31
PEACE	43
PERFECTION	50
PROVISION	57
PRIZE	63

OUR PLACE IN GOD THROUGH JESUS: (1)

Position

We have been raised up to new life with Christ and now we are hidden in Him. That means our life without Christ is gone, and we have a fresh life that has crossed over from death to life and will not be condemned (John 5.24).

Once we realize that our **Position** has changed through Christ, we will begin to believe, think and act differently. There is no greater name on Earth than the Name of Jesus (Philippians 2.9), and we are now found inside and covered by the mighty Person Who embodies this Name, Jesus!

> "Since you have **been raised to new life** with Christ, set your sights on the realities of heaven, where Christ sits in the place of

> honor at God's right hand...For you died to this life, and your real life is hidden with Christ in God" (Colossians 3:1 & 3 NLT).

God's Children

Not only has our new **Position** placed us in Christ, but we are also now positioned as **Children of God** instead of His enemy (Colossians 1.21). As His Children, God wants us to have His best blessings possible (Matthew 7.11). He is not far from us. He is near to us and eager to have a deepening relationship with us. No longer are we outsiders. We are now positioned in God's royal family.

> "But to all who believed him and accepted him, he gave the right to become **children of God**" (John 1.12 NLT).

This new position as God's Children also entails more awe-inspiring aspects that, when we fully understand and embrace them, will transform our minds, hearts and lives. As God's children, we are **Chosen**, **Royalty**, a **Priesthood**, **Holy**—and we **Belong**. We do not have to live in darkness any longer because God has positioned us in His wonderful light!

> "But you are not like that, for you are a chosen people. You are **royal priests**, a **holy nation**, God's very own **possession**. As a result, you can show others the goodness of God, for he called you out of the **darkness into his wonderful light**" (1 Peter 2.9 NLT).

How can we possibly live in defeat from a **Position** of such noble heritage? The glorious realities of our change in **Position** are limitless, but the following are just a few more positional qualities we gain in Christ.

Positional Qualities Gained in Christ

- **Victorious:** 1 Corinthians 15:57 (NLT)

"But thank God! He gives us **victory** over sin and death through our Lord Jesus Christ."

- **Righteous:** 2 Corinthians 5:21 (NKJV)

"For He made Him who knew no sin *to be* sin for us, that we might become the righteousness of God in Him."

- **The Head, not the Tail:** Deuteronomy 28:13 (NLT)

"If you listen to these commands of the Lord your God that I am giving you today, and if you carefully obey them, the Lord will make you the **head and not the tail**, and you will always be on top and never at the bottom."

- **Beloved:** Romans 1.7 (NKJV)

"To all who are in Rome, **beloved** of God, called *to be* saints: Grace to you and peace from God our Father and the Lord Jesus Christ."

- **Complete:** Colossians 2.10 (NLT)

"So you also are **complete** through your union with Christ, who is the head over every ruler and authority."

- **Perfected:** Hebrews 10.14 (NLT)

"For by that one offering he forever made **perfect** those who are being made holy."

- **Overcomer:** Revelation 12:11 (NKJV)

Alisa Hope Wagner | Our Place in God Through Jesus

"And they **overcame** him by the blood of the Lamb and by the word of their testimony, and they did not love their lives to the death."

Therefore, in Christ, we have been gifted a **Position** as **Royal Children of God** found as a **Holy, Chosen, Victorious, Righteous, Beloved, Complete, Perfected Priesthood** who **Overcome** all obstacles becoming the **Head, not the Tail,** because we **Belong** to our Loving Father!

Once the truth of our **Position** finally sinks into our hearts and minds, we can live out our true identity in Christ.

OUR PLACE IN GOD THROUGH JESUS: (2)

Purpose

"And we know that all things work together for good to those who love God, to those who are the called according to *His* **purpose**" (Romans 8.28 NKJV).

Now that we understand our **Position** in God, we can examine our **Purpose** in God. To have a **Purpose** on Earth is vital to our daily life. The Bible says that if we don't have a vision for our lives, we (our destinies) will perish. We have to know that our lives have meaning and that we fulfill a valuable service on Earth. The work we do must earn us more than a paycheck. It must fulfill our very real and strong desire to feel valuable, needed and prosperous. God is a creative God, and He has a creative **Purpose** for each of His children.

> "Where there is **no vision, the people perish:** but he that keepeth the law, happy is he" (Proverbs 29.18 KJV).

We have been created to do the will of God which will produce good works in our lives that line up with His Greater Kingdom Plan. Our **Purpose** is what keeps us walking by faith and trusting and relying on God in everything we do. Many times, God calls us to stretch our comfort zones and do things that scare us or seem impossible, and the reason we overcome our fears and make a leap of faith is that our **Purpose** draws us to continue despite feeling inadequate or not knowing the outcome.

> "For we are His workmanship, created in **Christ Jesus for good works,** which God prepared beforehand that we should walk in them" (Ephesians 2.10 NKJV).

When we get to Heaven we will be judged not by our sins because they have been cleansed by the Blood of Jesus. However, we will be judged based on what we did with the gifts and talents God wove into our nature in order to accomplish the **Purpose** He has for us. This **Purpose** will always serve the needs of others and quench our thirst for a life of meaning.

When we obey in our work according to God's will for us, we will one day hear Jesus say, "Well done!"

> "The master said, '**Well done, my good and faithful servant.** You have been faithful in handling this small amount, so now I will give you many more responsibilities. Let's celebrate together!'" (Matthew 25.23 NLT).

Our **Purpose** also brings us closer to God's best design for our lives. In order to achieve the great things God has planned for us, we must make a habit of learning, growing, stretching and relying on Him. Without a **Purpose**, there would be no reason to press forward and develop as individuals into the image of Christ. Christ completed the ultimate **Purpose** of reconciling the world back to God through His Finished Work on the Cross. Now it is our turn to pick up our own Cross—our personal **Purpose**—and follow the leading of the Holy Spirit (Matthew 16:24).

> "So all of us who have had that veil removed can see and reflect the glory of the Lord. And the Lord—who is the Spirit—makes us more and **more like him as we are changed into his glorious image**" (2 Corinthians 3.18 NLT).

If God didn't have a **Purpose** for our lives on Earth, He would simply take us straight to Heaven after we receive salvation through Jesus Christ. However, God does not take us up right away because He has a **Purpose** for our lives on Earth that will bless His Children and grow our maturity in Christ. Once we know our **Position** in God through Christ, we can ask God what **Purpose** He has for us, so we can align ourselves with God's Kingdom **Purpose.**

> "Declaring the end *and* the result from the beginning, And from ancient times the things which have not [yet] been done, Saying, '**My purpose** will be established, and I will do all that pleases Me *and* fulfills **My purpose**'" (Isaiah 46.10 AMP).

Below is a prayer we can say in order to ask God to reveal our **Purpose**, so we can begin living a life overflowing with meaning, value and blessing.

*"Dear Heavenly Father, now that I know my **Position** as a Child of God, I desire to know why I am here on this Earth, in this body, during this time and with the talents and gifts I've been born with and want to cultivate. God, reveal your great **Purpose** for my life to me. I want my steps each day to be directed by a*

*greater vision than I could have ever imagined. Open my eyes to all your plans, so I can wake up each day knowing I have worth, value and meaning. I now have a **Purpose** that will shine before others, and I can't wait to walk in my **Purpose** filled with great deeds that will glorify You. I pray this in Jesus' Name, Amen."*

> "In the same way, **let your light shine** before others, that they may see your good deeds and **glorify your Father** in heaven" (Matthew 5.16 NIV).

OUR PLACE IN GOD THROUGH JESUS: (3)

Promise

"For all of God's **promises** have been fulfilled in Christ with a resounding 'Yes!' And through Christ, our 'Amen' (which means 'Yes') ascends to God for his glory" (2 Corinthians 1.20 NLT).

Now that we know our **Position** in God as His Children and we have gained an understanding of our **Purpose**, we can now focus on the **Promise** God gives us to achieve all that He has planned. God's **Promises** will almost always seem impossible for us to achieve on our own. God places our promises at the foot of His throne, so as we walk toward them, we come closer into relationship with Him. And, yes, our **Promises** may be impossible, but with God all things are possible, which is why we must learn to trust and rely on His great hand to accomplish His **Promise** through us.

> "Jesus looked at them and said, 'With man this is impossible, but with God all things are possible'" (Matthew 19.26 NIV).

Once God gives us a **Promise**, we must write it down and claim it by faith daily. We can believe in the **Promise** despite our circumstances because many times our circumstances will be the complete opposite of our **Promise**. God allows this contradiction to produce faith in us. Our faith illustrates that we believe God above what our eyes see: "For we live by faith, not by sight" (2 Corinthians 5.7 NIV). As we collect God's **Promises** for our lives, we can trust that they will "surely come." Then once God accomplishes a **Promise**, it will become a testimony of our faith and God's grace. Plus, our faith will be boosted for the next **Promise** God has in store for us.

> "Then the Lord answered me and said: '**Write the vision** And make *it* plain on tablets, That he may run who reads it. For the vision *is* yet for an appointed time; But at the end it will speak, and it will not lie.

> Though it tarries, wait for it; **Because it will surely come,** It will not tarry'" (Habakkuk 2.2-3 NKJV).

The **Promises** of God make our **Purpose** possible. They also become motivators for us and endow our work with meaning, filling us with passion for the things of God. These **Promises** are like unopened gifts just waiting to be revealed and used to bless us and others. Jesus Himself was the first Gift given to us (John 4.10), and once the Gift of Salvation has been secured by faith, we can ask God to shed light on all the gifts He has in store for us in every season of life.

> "Every good thing given and **every perfect gift is from above**, coming down from the Father of Lights [the Creator and Sustainer of the heavens], in whom there is no variation [no rising or setting] or shadow cast by His turning [for He is perfect and never changes]" (James 1.17 AMP).

Jesus gave us a word of assurance that will help us believe, claim and achieve all the **Promises** of God for us. He said if we have faith as small as a mustard seed, nothing would be impossible for us. That single **Promise** should usurp all our fears. However, many times our **Promises** must die in the natural, so God can resurrect them in the supernatural. We can do our part, but there will be a point where we are going to have to lay the **Promises** of God at His feet and allow His strong arm to move on our behalf.

> "...Jesus told them. 'I tell you the truth, if you had faith even as sma**ll as a mustard seed**, you could say to this mountain, 'Move from here to there,' and it would move. Nothing would be impossible'" (Matthew 17.20 NLT).

Sometimes trusting God and waiting on His timing can be the most difficult actions to take. It will be tempting to go around God and achieve a lesser **Promise**. Or we may try to force His **Promise** in our own meager way. But whatever is achieved in our own strength must be maintained by our strength. What God achieves in His strength on our behalf will be maintained by His strength, and we will have a "holy ease" when walking in our **Promises**. God lives outside of time. Time doesn't matter as much as life matters. God will hold our **Promises** safely until He knows the greatest good will come out of them, and more often than not that takes time. But we don't have to be dismayed. We can simply trust that God always keeps His **Promises** no matter if they take days, weeks, months, years or even decades to come to fruition.

> "The Lord always keeps his promises; he is gracious in all he does" (Psalm 145.13b NLT).

We must not let discouragement prevent us from achieving all that God has **Promised** us. A day can be like a thousand years to God, so we must carry the weight of hope with great anticipation, renewing our faith whenever discouragement rears its ugly head.

> "But you must not forget this one thing, dear friends: **A day is like a thousand years to the Lord**, and a thousand years is like a day. The Lord isn't really being slow about his **promise**, as some people think. No, he is being patient for your sake. He does not want anyone to be destroyed, but wants everyone to repent" (2 Peter 3.8-9 NLT).

If you have lost faith in the **Promises** of God for your life, speak the prayer below by faith and trust that God is true to His Word.

*"Father God, You have given me many **Promises**. Some of them have come to pass and others I am still working toward and believing for. I declare today that Your Word is more powerful than my situation. By faith, I claim my **Promises** are 'Yes" and "Amen" in Christ. I will not speak a word against them. I will not believe the contradictions of my circumstances. I will only claim and speak each of my **Promises** as if they are already on Earth as they are in Heaven. I rebuke doubt. I rebuke fear. I rebuke discouragement. I rebuke worry. And I rebuke any hindering and distracting spirit that may be trying to work against my **Promises** from coming to fruition. I thank You, God, in advance for resurrecting my **Promises** in Your strength and time. I pray this in Jesus' name, Amen."*

> "Now all glory to God, who is able, through his mighty power at work within us, to **accomplish infinitely more than we might ask or think**" (Ephesians 3.20 NLT).

OUR PLACE IN GOD THROUGH JESUS: (4)

"I want to know Christ and experience the mighty **power** that raised him from the dead. I want to suffer with him, sharing in his death, so that one way or another I will experience the resurrection from the dead!" (Philippians 3.10-11 NLT).

God's ways are definitely not our ways (Isaiah 55.8-9). One would think to gain **Powe**r, we would have to fight for it: Read more. Meditate more. Study more. Work more. Though there is nothing wrong with these activities, they won't give us God's **Power.**

God Does Things Differently

We gain His **Power** by dying to self (our desires, our control, our ways) and submitting to God with complete abandonment like little children (Matthew 18:2-4). Once we get out of the way, God can pour His **Power** over us—the same **Power** that can raise people from the dead both physically and spiritually. And this is the same **Power** that can raise our God-given **Promises** from the dead.

We have guaranteed **Promises** from God extended to us by His grace and claimed by us with faith. However, these **Promises** are only attainable through God's **Power** working in our lives. God gives us a beautiful truth that when we stop focusing on our inabilities and begin focusing on His strength, His **Power** will flow mightily through us. Gaining **Power** is not about what we can offer; it's about what we are willing to receive by faith.

> "But he said to me, 'My grace is sufficient for you, for my **power** is made perfect in weakness.' Therefore I will boast all the more gladly of my weaknesses, so that the **power** of Christ may rest upon me. For the sake of Christ, then, I am content with

> weaknesses, insults, hardships, persecutions, and calamities. For when I am weak, then I am strong" (2 Corinthians 12.9-10 ESV).

How wonderful to know that it is our weakness that sparks His **Power** in us! Yes, we can work in our personal strengths, but those won't necessarily spur God's **Power.** God gets all the glory by moving in areas where we struggle because the workings of His **Power** are attributed to Him alone, not us. When we take steps of faith in our weakness, despite the unknowns and our insecurities, God steps up and moves His mighty arm on our behalf.

The world needs to see Christians walk with **Power**, not fear, anxiety, worry, insecurity, lack, discouragement, defeat, etc. We have the King of Kings on our side, wanting to wield His **Power** through us. That is what the world needs to see. A **Power** that can't come from a man or woman. A **Power** that can only come from a supernatural Source. This **Power** is ours for the taking. We simply need to tap into it. How do we gain this **Power**? It comes through salvation via the Cross of Christ.

> "For the word of the cross is folly to those who are perishing, but to us who are being saved it is the **power** of God" (1 Corinthians 1.18 ESV).

Jesus died, taking our sins with Him, and He rose three days later leaving our sins in the tomb. We are free from the trap of sin that tries to steal the **Power** we have in Jesus. Once our minds and hearts fully believe the truth of what Jesus' Finished Work accomplished for us, we can start walking in the **Power** we receive when the Holy Spirit—God's Spirit—unleashed onto the world on Pentecost. This **Power** came suddenly. The disciples couldn't earn it. This **Power** was a free gift given to us because Jesus swapped our sins for His righteousness and now the Holy Spirit can dwell within us along with His **Power.** However, we must believe this **Power** is ours by faith (1 Corinthians 2.5).

> "But you will receive **power** when the Holy Spirit comes on you; and you will be my witnesses in Jerusalem, and in all Judea and Samaria, and to the ends of the earth" (Acts 1.8 NIV).

It is time we ask the Holy Spirit for His **Power** to manifest in and around us. We have the Kingdom of God within us (Luke 17.20-21). And this Kingdom is best expressed with God's **Power** flowing in our lives. Words are not enough. Knowledge is not enough. With the **Power** of God on our side, all things are possible, and we can overcome every obstacle, difficulty, heartache and enemy (Matthew 19.26). Once we free ourselves with the **Power** of God, we can help free others.

> "For the kingdom of God is not a matter of talk but of **power**" (1 Corinthians 4.20 NIV).

God wants us to have His **Power**. He sent His Son to the Cross not only to save us but to give us His **Power** on Earth to do mighty works according to His Kingdom Plan. We have the **Power** of God at our fingertips, so we should be the most confident, brave and daring people in Christ.

We can walk boldly by faith, trusting that God's **Power** will make a way where there is no way, will accomplish all God's **Promises** for us and will break through the enemy's forces in order to gain more territory for the Kingdom of God.

"I also pray that you will understand the incredible greatness of God's **power** for us who believe him. This is the same mighty **power** that raised Christ from the dead and seated him in the place of honor at God's right hand in the heavenly realms" (Ephesians 1:19-20 NLT).

OUR PLACE IN GOD THROUGH JESUS: (5)

Protection

"I give them eternal life, and they shall never perish; no one will **snatch them out of my hand**" (John 10.28 NIV).

God gives us the ultimate **Protection:** Through Jesus' Finished Work on the Cross, we have been reconciled back to God—and no one can snatch us out of God's hands. Once we accept Jesus as our Lord and Savior, our eternity with Him is sealed. A contract has been made via God's grace and our faith and signed with the Blood of Jesus Christ, the Messiah. Our salvation is set in stone. That truth in itself is enough to give us profound daily joy. Life has its troubles, heartache and pain—but in eternity there will be no more tears, sorrow, pain or death.

> "He will wipe every tear from their eyes, and there will be **no more death or sorrow or crying or pain.** All these things are gone forever" (Revelation 21.4 NLT).

With God's **Power** on our side, the enemy is going to step up his game to steal our destiny, destroy our testimony and kill our faith (John 10.10). However, we do not have to live in fear because God grants us not just **Protection** of our spirits, but **Protection** according to His will in our lives and our faithfulness to him. God is a good Father, and He wants His Children to have **Protection.** Yes, the world has fallen from God's best and sin entered the Earth. God's Children make mistakes, hurt others and even do unthinkable atrocities. However, as a Child of the King, I would like to believe that God is looking out for us. We want to always be aware and expectant of His divine intervention on our behalf.

> "He guards the paths of the just and **protects** those who are faithful to him" (Proverbs 2.8 NLT).

In the Garden of Eden, God created two trees. The Tree of Knowledge of Good and Evil represents our free will to choose to obey God or disobey Him. If we didn't have free will, we wouldn't truly be children made in the image of a creative God. God gave us the gift of free will to create beauty, but this gift came with a price. We can also use this free will to create ugliness, which is why God added one more tree in the Garden of Eden: The Tree of Life. The Tree of Life is the redemption plan for the mistakes we would make with our free will. The Tree of Life is Jesus Christ Who with His sacrifice and resurrection wipes clean our sins and perfects everything we create for His glory to His holy standard.

> "The Lord God made all sorts of trees grow up from the ground—trees that were beautiful and that produced delicious fruit. In the middle of the garden he placed the **tree of life** and the **tree of the knowledge of good and evil**" (Genesis 2.9 NLT).

Out of God's great love for us, He created people made in His image, gave them free will to be free-thinking individuals and He sent Himself into the world in the form of Jesus Christ to die for the evil we commit with our free will. The alternative would be not to create children at all, but aren't we glad He didn't let our mistakes stop Him from creating and loving us so much (John 3.16)? And not only that, but He also declares that He will be our safe refuge and our fortress as we put our trust in Him. He will be our ultimate **Protector.**

> "He who dwells in the secret place of the Most High Shall abide under the shadow of the Almighty. I will say of the Lord, '***He is* my refuge and my fortress**; My God, in Him I will trust'" (Psalm 91.1-2 NKJV).

Yet, bad things still happen. We still get hurt. People still commit wrongs against us. Where is God's **Protection** there? His **Protection** comes in two parts: **Protection and Redemption** (Psalms 19.14). God says that when we do go through hard times, He will heal us. He also says that though we may weep at night, joy will surely come in the morning.

> "He **heals the brokenhearted and binds up their wounds**" (Psalm 147.3 NIV).

> "...Weeping may last through the night, but **joy comes with the morning**" (Psalm 30.5b NLT).

The truth of the matter is that trials and tribulations grow us, make us strong and bring us closer to God. Every good writer and movie maker knows that there must be conflict in the story in order for the protagonist to transform his or her character with greater integrity, love, diligence and compassion. Just like going to the gym to lift weights, God allows resistance in our lives to bulk up our spiritual muscles because we are becoming the people we will be for eternity. We must never run from conflict. Instead, we head straight into the storm knowing that our miracle-making Faither in Heaven is with us and working according to our faith in Him. Part of trusting God's **Protection** is facing challenges, believing that God will provide a way for us to endure.

> "No temptation has overtaken you except what is common to mankind. And God is faithful; he will not let you be tempted beyond what you can bear. But when you are tempted, **he will also provide a way out so that you can endure it**" (1 Corinthians 10.13 NIV).

God gives us another beautiful declaration of His **Protection**, which may seem like an oxymoron at first. He says we will suffer, but that suffering will produce a good work in us that is more valuable than anything the world can offer us. A comfortable life will never be a life of victory because heroes are made when they overcome adversaries, struggles and temptations. God's **Protection** comes in the form of being a Father Who wants His Children not to simply survive but thrive. And we thrive understanding that, yes, we will face difficulties, but we have the King of Kings and Lord of Lords walking with us every step of the way. We can put our hope in the truth that He is producing a valuable and eternal harvest of goodness in our lives.

> "Not only this, but we also rejoice in sufferings, **knowing that suffering produces endurance, and endurance, character, and character, hope. And hope does not disappoint,** because the love of God has been poured out in our hearts through the Holy Spirit who was given to us" (Romans 5.3-5 NET).

Finally, no matter the craziness of this world, we can still believe God is with us, **Protecting** us every step of the way. And we can use our words filled with faith to claim His **Protection.** Plus, we can pray

Protection over our families and friends, over our travels, over our churches, over our countries, etc. Our words of faith penetrate the supernatural world and shape the physical world around us.

One example of declaring God's **Protection** is if we take a hike down a grueling path. As we walk, we can pray Psalm 116.8: "For You have rescued my life from death, My eyes from tears, **And my feet from stumbling *and* falling**" (AMP). All of God's **Promises** found in the Bible are potentially ours. We simply need to believe them and claim them, so let us start claiming God's divine **Protection.**

Here are just a few of God's promises of **Protection** from the Bible. Claim them when flying in a plane. Claim them when children play sports. Claim them when a spouse is running late to prevent worry. Be proactive and claim God's **Protection** daily. Our faith-words can move mountains, so they can surely affect the situation and people around us (Matthew 17.20-21).

- "But the Lord is faithful, and he will strengthen you and **protect** you from the evil one" (2 Thessalonians 3.3 NIV).

- "Then I, myself, will be a **protective** wall of fire around Jerusalem, says the LORD. And I will be the glory inside the city!" (Zechariah 2.5 NLT).
- "Pull me from the trap my enemies set for me, for I find **protection** in you alone" (Psalm 31.4 NLT).
- "I have given you authority to trample on snakes and scorpions and to overcome all the power of the enemy; **nothing will harm you**" (Luke 10.19 NIV).
- "But let all who take refuge in you rejoice; let them sing joyful praises forever. Spread your **protection** over them, that all who love your name may be filled with joy" (Psalm 5.11 NLT).
- "Have I not commanded you? Be strong and courageous. Do not be afraid; do not be discouraged, for the **Lord your God will be with you wherever you go**" (Joshua 1.9 NIV).

OUR PLACE IN GOD THROUGH JESUS: (6)

Prosperity is a tricky word in Christian culture today. It almost seems like a bad word, but our **Place** in God is to **Prosper**—growing, not decreasing. The question is that if we are not **Prospering** in our resources, finances, relationships, spirituality, knowledge, character, love, faith, health, etc., how will we be a mighty force for the Kingdom of God and gain ground for His will to reach people with His love? **Prosperity** is simply not financial. The Bible makes it clear that we can **Prosper** in EVERY WAY!

> "Beloved, I pray that in **every way** you may succeed *and* **prosper** and be in good health [physically], just as [I know] your soul **prospers** [spiritually]" (3 John 1.2 AMP).

Some critics of **Prosperity** cite the Bible story of the Rich Young Ruler's interaction with Jesus as a reason to be poor. However, this is taking a single Bible verse out of context without comparing it to other verses. The reason Jesus told this particular young man to sell all He had and follow Him was because money was a stronghold in his life.

> "Jesus said to him, 'If you want to be perfect, **go, sell what you have and give to the poor,** and you will have treasure in heaven; and come, follow Me'" (Matthew 19.21 NKJV).

The young man walked away sad because he was extremely wealthy (v. 22). He wouldn't give the money up, and it became an idol in his life, causing him to miss the wonderful things of God. But what if the young man did obey? God could have easily blessed the young man with double his wealth because now he could be trusted to be a good steward of the money and not overshadow his love of God.

When Jesus encountered Zacchaeus—a tax collector who was also very rich—Jesus never asked him to sell all his possessions. Rather, Zacchaeus volunteered to give up half his money to the poor.

> "Then Zacchaeus stood and said to the Lord, 'Look, Lord, **I give half of my goods to the poor**; and if I have taken anything from anyone by false accusation, I restore fourfold'" (Luke 19.8 NKJV).

Half is definitely not ALL like Jesus asked from the Rich Young Ruler, yet Jesus told Zacchaeus and the crowd around them that "Today salvation has come to this [Zacchaeus's] house, because he also is a son of Abraham; for the Son of Man has come to seek and to save that which was lost" (Luke 19.9 NKJV). Zacchaeus gave half of all he owned, and salvation entered his home and life. He wanted salvation more than he wanted money. Money may have once been an idol in Zacchaeus's life but no more. Now he put God first.

The truth about Jesus is that He can read the hearts of all people: "and He [Jesus] did not need anyone to testify concerning man [and human nature], for He **Himself knew what was in man [in their hearts—in the very core of their being]**" (John 2.25 AMP).

His interactions with people varied, but His Love, Truth and Destiny were immovable. Just like a good parent or teacher knows, we can't treat everyone the same because our love for him or her moves in equally powerful yet uniquely different ways according to the individual's needs, experiences, strengths, weaknesses and personalities. We are each designed differently, so we can't have a cookie-cutter way of interacting with others.

Another example of this variance of interactions is found in Luke Chapter 8 when the woman with the issue of blood for twelve years touched Jesus's garment and was healed. There was a great crowd around them, and Jesus stopped everything to find out who received power from Him. When she was discovered, He showcased her and her healing to the multitude. He would not allow her or the miracle that she received to stay hidden.

> "When the woman realized that **she could not stay hidden**, she began to tremble and fell to her knees in front of him. The **whole crowd heard her** explain why she had touched him and that she had been immediately healed. 'Daughter,' he said to her, 'your faith has made you well. Go in peace'" (Luke 8.47-48 NLT).

But right after He heals the woman with the issue of blood, Jesus goes into Jairus's home and heals his twelve-year-old daughter. But this time Jesus wants the miracle to stay hidden. Jesus actually insisted that her parents tell absolutely no one about the healing.

> "Her parents were overwhelmed, but **Jesus insisted that they not tell anyone what had happened**" (Luke 8.56 NLT).

Who knows why Jesus would keep one miracle hidden and another exposed? Why did Jesus tell one man to tell no one (other than the priest to be cleaned) of his healing (Matthew 8.4), yet He told another man to go back to his people and tell everyone what the Lord has done (Mark 5.19)? There is plenty of speculation, but the main conclusion is that Jesus was obeying the Father's will. Therefore, He can tell one person to sell all their possessions and allow another person—who has learned to be obedient with money—to keep half his wealth to further the Kingdom. Either way, the will of the Father was being obeyed.

> "So Jesus said to them, 'Truly, truly, I say to you, the **Son can do nothing of his own**

> **accord, but only what he sees the Father doing.** For whatever the Father does, that the Son does likewise'" (John 5.19 ESV).
>
> Another verse taken out of context concerning **Prosperity** is the following: "For the **love of money is a root of all kinds of evils**. It is through this craving that some have wandered away from the faith and pierced themselves with many pangs" (1 Timothy 6.10 ESV).

This verse doesn't say money is evil. Plenty of people in the Bible had wealth: Job, Noah (he had enough money for materials and workers to build a huge ark to be the home for his family and the world's animals for months), Abraham, Joseph (second in command of the richest nation of his time), King David and Queen Esther. Queen Esther was willing to risk her position as queen and her very life to obey the will of God. These biblical figures used their wealth in obedience to God to the best of their abilities. Money isn't evil. In fact, it can and is being used for great good on Earth.

The problem comes—just like with the Young Rich Ruler—when we **put money above God.** Money gives us power, and if we are not aligned with God's heart, we will use it for evil not good. There is evidence all around us today of money being used for evil. But there is also evidence all around us of money being used for good. Money can be used to support ministries and charities that bring the Good News of Jesus Christ to the world along with providing basic needs of life: water, food, shelter, clothing, medical care and information.

Moreover, money can be used in personal interactions with people in order for them to have a tangible experience of the goodness of God. This can especially be seen in Jesus's parable about the **Good Samaritan** (Luke 10.25-27).

A man lay dying on the side of the road. The Priest and Levite both offer him no help and pass him by. Yet, a Samaritan stops and helps him. The Samaritan brings the dying man to an innkeeper and pays him to take care of the dying man. Without wealth, the story of the **Good Samaritan** would not be possible. The Samaritan needed a surplus in order to provide for the dying man.

We can't offer help to others if we can't even take care of our own needs. This means we need an overflow of resources that supersedes our lifestyle expenses. And this overflow will vary depending on each individual and every season of life. Yes, sometimes the overflow takes time because we are investing in our future, in our business and in our education; but eventually, we should be gaining, not decreasing. And even if we do lose it all, as Job in the Bible did, we can trust that God will redeem our situation with His abundance as we follow and obey Him.

The final point of our **Place** of **Prosperity** in God is that to be **Prosperous**, we must be **Generous**. We must give God His tithe. Then we can give above our tithe with offerings to the works of God on Earth that we are passionate about. We can be generous with the people around us, trusting that God's supply is limitless. ***The less our hands hold tightly onto money, the more God can pour His resources into our open palms.***

> "'**Bring the whole tithe into the storehouse,** that there may be food in my house. Test me in this,' says the Lord Almighty, 'and **see if I will not throw open the floodgates of heaven and pour out so much blessing that**

there will not be room enough to store it'" (Malachi 3.10 NIV).

The following verses will help us better understand what it is to have a **Prosperous Place** in God, growing in **ALL** areas of life, not just money.

- "But **grow** in the grace and knowledge of our Lord and Savior Jesus Christ. To him be the glory both now and to the day of eternity. Amen" (2 Peter 3.18 ESV).
- "**Give, and it will be given to you.** A good measure, pressed down, shaken together and running over, will be poured into your lap. For with the measure you use, it will be measured to you" (Luke 6.38 NIV).
- "The point is this: whoever sows sparingly will also reap sparingly, and **whoever sows bountifully will also reap bountifully**" (2 Corinthians 9.6 ESV).
- "The **generous man [is a source of blessing and] shall be prosperous *and* enriched**, And he who waters will himself be watered [reaping the generosity he has sown]" (Proverbs 11.25 AMP).
- "You will be **enriched in every way so that you may be generous**, and this [generosity,

administered] through us is producing thanksgiving to God [from those who benefit]" (2 Corinthians 9.11 AMP).
- "But seek first his kingdom and his righteousness, and **all these things will be given to you** as well" (Matthew 6.33 NIV).
- "If any of you lacks wisdom, you should ask God, **who gives generously to all** without finding fault, and it will be given to you" (James 1.5 NIV).
- "If you then, though you are evil, know how to give good gifts to your children, how much more will **your Father in heaven give the Holy Spirit to those who ask him**!" (Luke 11.13 NIV).
- "You did not choose me, but I chose you and appointed you that **you should go and bear fruit and that your fruit should abide**, so that whatever you ask the Father in my name, he may give it to you" (John 15.16 ESV).
- "Be generous: Invest in acts of charity. **Charity yields high returns**" (Ecclesiastes 11.1 MSG).
- "Instead, we will speak the truth in love, **growing in every way more and more like**

Christ, who is the head of his body, the church" (Ephesians 4.15 NLT).

Sometimes, God will ask us to give up something (to be generous), and our blessing will come back to us in another form. The story of **The Widow's Offering** is a wonderful example of this (Mark 12:41-44). This widow gave the very last she had (only a few cents) to God. And what she received in return was eternal and priceless. Jesus (the Son of God) mentioned her to His disciples as a learning lesson, and her story is written in the Holy Spirit Inspired Book of the Bible. Now, her step of obedience has influenced countless lives throughout history. That is way better than gold and silver!

Often, our generosity doesn't return to us as we thought it would, but God's ways are not our ways (Isaiah 55.8-9). And we can trust that if we are obedient, God sees and will reward us either in this life or the next (Matthew 6.4). Money is meant to be used for good. And as we use it to bless our families, others and our churches, we can trust that we are building up an even better treasure in Heaven that time can never take away from us. As we love God and others, our **Prosperity** will be a blessing in the Kingdom of God.

"Do not store up for yourselves treasures on earth, where moths and vermin destroy, and where thieves break in and steal. **But store up for yourselves treasures in heaven**, where moths and vermin do not destroy, and where thieves do not break in and steal. For **where your treasure is, there your heart will be also**" (Matthew 6.19-21 NIV).

OUR PLACE IN GOD THROUGH JESUS: (7)

Peace

"For to us a child is born, to us a son is given, and the government will be on his shoulders. And he will be called Wonderful Counselor, Mighty God, Everlasting Father, **Prince of Peace**. Of the greatness of his government and **peace there will be no end**. He will reign on David's throne and over his kingdom, establishing and upholding it with justice and righteousness from that time on and forever. The zeal of the Lord Almighty will accomplish this" (Isaiah 9.6-7 NIV).

One of Jesus's main objectives in coming to the Earth was not only to offer us salvation through His Finished Work on the Cross, but to finally offer us true and lasting **Peace**.

How? We have been reconciled back to God through Jesus (Romans 5.10-11), and God is the **Author of Peace: "For God is not** *the author* **of confusion but of peace**, as in all the churches of the saints" (1 Corinthians 14.33 NKJV). God, as the **Author of Peace**, surrounds and fills us with His **Perfect Peace** as we learn to trust in Him and grow in our intimacy with His presence. This **Peace** can't be bought or received through any human or earthly means. It only comes through a relationship with God through the Cross.

> "And let the **peace that comes from Christ** rule in your hearts. For as members of one body you are called to live in peace. And always be thankful" (Colossians 3.15 NLT).

God's **Peace** is a supernatural exchange for our anxiety, confusion, worry, fear, doubt, etc., and this **Peace** takes a believing faith to receive. God's **Peace** is a truth found in His Word. We must acknowledge this truth, believe it and walk in it. We don't have to ask for it because it is already ours to claim by faith through Jesus Christ. We simply say, "I have complete **Peace** in Christ," over and over again until that truth moves from our minds to our hearts. Jesus told us that He has left us His **Peace** before His ascension to the right-hand side of the Father after His death and resurrection (1 Peter 3.22). His **Peace** is a gift that is already here on Earth for us to grab hold of and to experience.

> "I am leaving you with a gift—**peace of mind and heart**. And the **peace I give is a gift** the world cannot give. So don't be troubled or afraid" (John 14.27 NLT).

Yes, life will have storms. Just like Jesus sleeping in the boat while the wind and waves stormed around Him, we can have Peace regardless of the storms in our life because we know that God is with us. Jesus demonstrated that it takes faith to choose **Peace** over fear when He rebuked His disciples for showing a lack of faith when they feared: "You of little faith, why are you so afraid?" (Matthew 8.26a NIV).

By this time, the disciples had seen Jesus do many miracles. Just before the storm, Jesus had healed a man with leprosy, healed the Centurion's servant, healed Peter's mother-in-law and healed many who were demon-possessed (Matthew 8.1-27). If Jesus could accomplish those miracles, He could accomplish anything—even calming the storm—because He has overcome the world for us.

> "I have told you all this so that you may have **peace** in me. Here on earth you will have many trials and sorrows. But take heart, because **I have overcome the world**" (John 16.33 NLT).

Many times, we fear because we are facing a new storm. We have seen God's hand working in stormy times before; however, this new situation is nothing like we've ever experienced. It is in those moments that we need to pour our faith from God's previous miraculous works in our life into the new circumstance. The disciples may have never experienced a storm that fierce before, so they needed to pour their faith from the previous times Jesus miraculously moved and place it into the new situation of the storm. Pouring our faith into every new circumstance will ensure our **Peace**. The situation may seem scary at first, but we can trust that in every way, every situation and every trial, God gives us His **Peace** always.

> "Now may the Lord of peace Himself give you **peace always in every way.** The Lord *be* with you all" (2 Thessalonians 3.16 NKJV).

We can believe that just as Jesus made the storm completely calm, He can make our hearts and minds completely calm. However, it takes us choosing to embrace His **Peace** instead of embracing fear. God is in this "boat" with us. He will never leave nor forsake us, so we can be strong and courageous in this truth (Deuteronomy 31.6). Then we can be at **Peace**, knowing that we are not alone.

In fact, we have the King of the Universe on our side. There is nothing too hard for Him to accomplish (Genesis 18.14). Today, we can start claiming the **Peace** of God and rebuke fear, worry, anxiety, doubt, etc. Though the process of letting go of fear and taking hold of God's **Peace** may take some time, we can trust that if we keep at it, our minds will be renewed in Christ, and we can finally abide in His **Perfect Peace** (Romans 12.2).

Alisa Hope Wagner | Our Place in God Through Jesus

The following are 10 Bible verses with **Promises** of God's **Peace.**

- "I have told you all this so that you may have **peace** in me. Here on earth you will have many trials and sorrows. But take heart, because I have overcome the world" (John 16.33 NLT).
- "God the Father was pleased to have everything made perfect by Christ, His Son. Everything in heaven and on earth can come to God because of Christ's death on the cross. Christ's blood has made **peace**" (Colossians 1.19-20 NLV).
- "Therefore, since we have been justified by faith, we have **peace** with God through our Lord Jesus Christ" (Romans 5.1 ESV).
- "For he himself is our peace, who has made us both one and has broken down in his flesh the dividing wall of hostility by abolishing the law of commandments expressed in ordinances, that he might create in himself one new man in place of the two, so making **peace**, and might reconcile us both to God in one body through the cross, thereby killing the hostility" (Ephesians 2.14-16 ESV).

- "Therefore do not let your good be spoken of as evil; for the kingdom of God is not eating and drinking, but righteousness and **peace** and joy in the Holy Spirit" (Romans 14.16-17 NKJV).
- "You will keep *him* in perfect **peace**, *Whose* mind *is* stayed *on You,* Because he trusts in You" (Isaiah 26.3 NKJV).
- "But the Holy Spirit produces this kind of fruit in our lives: love, joy, **peace**, patience, kindness, goodness, faithfulness, gentleness, and self-control. There is no law against these things!" (Galatians 5.22-23 NLT).
- "You will keep in perfect **peace** those whose minds are steadfast, because they trust in you" (Isaiah 26.3 NIV).
- "The Lord gives his people strength. The Lord blesses them with **peace**" (Psalm 29.11 NLT).
- "But he was pierced for our transgressions, he was crushed for our iniquities; the punishment that brought us **peace** was on him, and by his wounds we are healed" (Isaiah 53.5 NIV).

OUR PLACE IN GOD THROUGH JESUS: (8)

Perfection

"But our High Priest offered himself to God as a single sacrifice for sins, good for all time. Then he sat down in the place of honor at God's right hand. There he waits until his enemies are humbled and made a footstool under his feet. For by that one offering he forever made **perfect** those who are being made holy" (Hebrews 10.12-14 NLT).

How can we possibly believe we have been made **Perfect** in Christ when we stumble and fall so often? The answer is simple. We are made up of three parts: Spirit, Soul (mind, heart and will) and Body. Once we accept Jesus as our Lord and Savior, it is the Spirit part of us that is **Perfected** through the

Finished Work of Jesus on the Cross. Our Spirit, which was once separated from God, has now passed from death to life, and we are reconciled back to God (John 5.25). This reconciliation can only come through the Cross of Christ. Jesus gave us His **Perfect** status with God, and He took our sinful status. Then He brought our sinful status with Him into death and rose from the grave three days later leaving that sinful status behind. He became our Holy and Final Sacrifice (Ephesians 5.2), erasing sin once and for all for those who accept His gift of salvation (1 John 1.7).

> "Much more then, having now been justified by His blood, we shall be saved from wrath through Him. For if when we were enemies **we were reconciled to God through the death of His Son**, much more, having been reconciled, we shall be saved by His life" (Romans 5.9-10 NKJV).

Therefore, the eternal part of us—our Spirit—has been made **Perfect**, so we can now have a relationship with God. Proof of our **Perfection** is the Holy Spirit (1 John 4.13). We gain the Holy Spirit within the seed of our **Perfected** Spirit. If we died today, our relationship with God would continue into Heaven through our Spirit. However, now the work of complete **Perfection** has only just begun. We want to work that **Perfection** into the other areas of our being, including our minds, hearts, wills and bodies. We want to submit all of our existence to that part of us that was made **Perfect** in Christ. This is what it means to be Spirit-led. We submit to the **Perfected** part of us that houses the Spirit of the Living God (1 Corinthians 6.19).

> "Not that I have already obtained it [this goal of being Christlike] or have already been made **perfect**, but I actively press on so that I may take hold of that [**perfection**] for which Christ Jesus took hold of me *and* made me His own. Brothers and sisters, I do not consider that I have made it my own yet; but one thing *I do*: forgetting what *lies* behind and reaching forward to what *lies* ahead" (Philippians 3.12-13 AMP).

The words above penned by the Apostle Paul may sound a bit confusing at first glance. Are we **Perfect** or not? He writes earlier in Philippians that we have been made righteous by faith (Philippians 3.8-9). Then he goes on to explain that Jesus took hold of us with His **Perfection** and made us His own. However, now it is our turn to take hold of Him and work His **Perfection** into all areas of our life. We have been **Perfected** in Christ, but it takes time for our hearts and minds to receive, believe and live in this truth. Paul writes that he hasn't achieved this complete **Perfection** yet, but he is actively reaching toward it.

We can actively reach toward it by allowing the **Perfected** part of us (our Spirit) to encompass the entirety of us. This is why we can both embody the **Perfection** of Christ and still work on gaining the **Perfection** of Christ in all areas of life. We can be confident of our **Perfection** by faith, realizing that the process of achieving **Perfection** in our minds, hearts, wills and bodies will take effort and time.

> "How foolish can you be? After starting your new lives in the Spirit, why are you now trying to become **perfect** by your own human effort?" (Galatians 3.3 NLT).

We cannot be **Perfect** in all areas in our *own efforts*. We need the Holy Spirit's guidance, grace and favor to lead us to the Perfection of Christ. It is by faith that our Spirit has been made **Perfect**, and it is by faith and obedience that we will walk in growing **Perfection**. Jesus did the hard part. He died to give us His **Perfection** that we receive by faith. Now all we need to do is keep our eyes on Him and walk in obedience to the guidance of the Holy Spirit within us (Acts 5.32). As we walk in faith daily, we will transform into the likeness of Christ from glory to glory (2 Corinthians 3.18).

> "Therefore you shall be **perfect**, just as your Father in heaven is **perfect**" (Matthew 5.48 NKJV).

Not only has our Spirit been made **Perfect**, and that **Perfection** is working its way into all areas of our life, but we also have a continuous **Perfecting** gift, as well. This **Perfecting** gift is the Blood of Jesus Christ, cleansing us of *all unrighteousness* continuously as we admit our wrongs to God. How amazing! When we stumble and fall, we can confess our sin, turn toward God and allow the Blood of Jesus to wash us clean. The Blood of Jesus can cleanse our minds, hearts, wills and bodies, bringing us into alignment with the **Perfect** standard of God. There are no hopeless scenarios with God. He has given us a 3-part **Place** of **Perfection** in Him through Jesus Christ. Our Spirit has been made **Perfect** by faith. That **Perfection** is working itself into all areas of life as we pursue the Holy Spirit, and we have the **Perfecting** Blood of Christ washing us clean.

> "But if we walk in the light, as he is in the light, we have fellowship with one another, and the blood of Jesus, his Son, purifies us from all sin. If we claim to be without sin, we deceive ourselves and the truth is not in us. **If we confess our sins, he is faithful and just and will forgive us our sins and purify us from all unrighteousness**" (1 John 1.7-9 NIV).

Here are seven verses about your Perfect Place in God through Christ.

- "In bringing many sons and daughters to glory, it was fitting that God, for whom and through whom everything exists, should make the pioneer of their salvation **perfect** through what he suffered" (Hebrews 2.10 NIV).

- "But may the God of all grace, who called us to His eternal glory by Christ Jesus, after you have suffered a while, **perfect**, establish, strengthen, and settle you" (1 Peter 5.10 NKJV).
- "But he said to me, 'My grace is sufficient for you, for my power is made **perfect** in weakness.' Therefore I will boast all the more gladly of my weaknesses, so that the power of Christ may rest upon me" (2 Corinthians 12.9 ESV).
- "For the upright shall dwell in the land, and the **perfect** shall remain in it" (Proverbs 2.21 KJV).
- "So let it grow, for when your endurance is fully developed, you will be **perfect** and complete, needing nothing" (James 1.4 NLT).
- "God arms me with strength, and he makes my way **perfect**" (Psalm 18.32 NLT).
- "For the law never made anything **perfect**. But now we have confidence in a better hope, through which we draw near to God" (Hebrews 7.19 NLT).

OUR PLACE IN GOD THROUGH JESUS: (9)

Provision

"Abraham looked up and there in a thicket he saw a ram caught by its horns. He went over and took the ram and sacrificed it as a burnt offering instead of his son. So Abraham called that place **The LORD Will Provide**. And to this day it is said, 'On the mountain of the LORD it will be provided'" (Genesis 22.13-14 NIV).

One of the names that Abraham gave God is *Yahweh Yireh*, which means "The LORD will Provide." The context of this **Provision** is so precious. God asked Abraham to sacrifice the very **Promise** he and his wife had waited for so long. And though they were beyond the age of childbearing, God did a miracle and **Provided** their son, Isaac, in their old age (Genesis 21.1-7). However, God asked Abraham to sacrifice this **Promise** to test his heart. Would Abraham put his realized **Promise** above God? Abraham knew he had a **Promise** of being a father to many nations (Genesis 17.4-6), and despite the contradiction of sacrificing the very person who was to be the continuation of this **Promise**, Abraham trusted God would **Provide**. When his son, Isaac, noted that they had the *wood* and *fire* but no sacrifice, Abraham answered, "God himself will **provide** the lamb for the burnt offering, my son" (Genesis 22.8 NIV).

> "He who did not spare his own Son, but gave him up for us all—how will he not also, along with him, **graciously give** us all things?" (Romans 8.32 NIV).

The story of God Providing a ram to be sacrificed instead of Isaac is a beautiful picture of God **Providing** Jesus to be sacrificed for us. And if God would **Provide** us with Jesus, His One Begotten Son (John 3.16), so we could be reconciled back to Him, what else would He not **graciously give**? Jesus is the

Ultimate **Provision**. Everything else is easy and simple for God to **Provide**. Our **Place** in God is a **Place** of **Provision**. Sometimes we miss this **Provision** because our ways are not His ways, but He will **Provide** for us in creative ways if we keep our spiritual eyes and ears seeking and listening (Isaiah 55.8-9). Sometimes that **Provision** will come instantly; however, many times that **Provision** will take years. Either way, we can continue to trust that God is outside of time, and He will **Provide** according to His will, not our timetable.

> "For God is the one who **provides** seed for the farmer and then bread to eat. In the same way, he will **provide** and increase your resources and then produce a great harvest of generosity in you" (2 Corinthians 9.10 NLT).

God wants to **Provide** graciously to us, but we must give Him seeds of faith that open a portal to His **Provision** from Heaven to Earth. Our words are so important. We must believe God will **Provide** and speak words of faith in His **Provision**. It is so easy to speak about the lack we see before us. However,

"...we live by faith, not by sight" (2 Corinthians 5.7 NIV). If we know that God has **Provided** His Son, we can trust that He can **Provide** all things "according to the riches of his glory in Christ Jesus" (Philippians 4.19 NIV). We must speak words of belief that God is actively **Providing** everything we need each day. No matter the bleakness of the situation, we can trust in the greatness of our God. Our words can bind things in our lives and loose things in our lives. So let us loose God's **Provision** and bind up the hindering spirit of the enemy.

> "Truly, I say to you, whatever you **bind** on earth shall be bound in heaven, and whatever you **loose** on earth shall be loosed in heaven" (Matthew 18.18 ESV).

Once we align our words with God's Provision, our actions must follow suit. When Abraham spoke words of faith that God would **Provide** a sacrifice, He also had to walk up the mountain in that belief and receive that **Provision**. Many times, we claim that God will **Provide,** but we don't move our feet according to our belief. If we are believing God for an honorable husband, we need to become an honorable wife. If we are believing God for financial breakthrough, we must take steps to learn and gain experience stewarding money. If we are believing God for a platform to share Christ with the world, we need to take time to get to know Him daily in our personal lives. Our actions must line up with our words which line up with our beliefs. God wants to **Provide**, but we need to take part in His **Provision.** Once we are overflowing with God's **Provision**, then we can share that abundance with the people of the world who are in need.

> "And God will generously **provide** all you need. Then you will always have everything you need and plenty left over to share with others" (2 Corinthians 9.8 NLT).

Here are seven more verses on Provision that we can speak by faith as we follow the Holy Spirit's leading in obedience.

- "The disciples, as each one was able, decided to **provide** help for the brothers and sisters living in Judea" (Acts 11.29 NIV).

- "The young lions lack and suffer hunger; But those who seek the Lord **shall not lack any good *thing***" (Psalm 34.10 NKJV).
- "So if you faithfully obey the commands I am giving you today—to love the Lord your God and to serve him with all your heart and with all your soul— then I will send rain on your land in its season, both autumn and spring rains, so that you may gather in your grain, new wine and olive oil. I will **provide** grass in the fields for your cattle, and you will eat and be satisfied" (Deuteronomy 11.13-15 NIV).
- "You **provide** a broad path for my feet, so that my ankles do not give way (Psalm 18.36 NIV).
- "**For He satisfies** the parched throat and fills the hungry appetite with what is good" (Psalm 107.9 AMP).
- "For the Lord God is our sun and our shield. He gives us grace and glory. The Lord will **withhold no good thing** from those who do what is right" (Psalm 84.11 NLT).

OUR PLACE IN GOD THROUGH JESUS: (10)

Prize

"Brothers and sisters, I do not consider myself yet to have taken hold of it. But one thing I do: Forgetting what is behind and straining toward what is ahead, I press on toward the goal to win the **prize** for which God has called me heavenward in Christ Jesus" (Philippians 3.13-14 NIV).

We have an assignment on Earth. Once we accept Jesus as our Lord and Savior, our life of faith is just beginning. There is a "race," as the Apostle Paul calls it during our time on Earth. And we want to run our race to win the **Prize**! The most brilliant aspect of this **Prize** is hearing Jesus say to us, "Well done, good and faithful servant!" (Matthew 25.23a NIV).

God has a race that we are guaranteed to win because it was created just for us. We have been given a **Purpose** that is part of God's greater plan. Each of us has our very own **Prize** waiting for us on the other side of our obedience and steadfastness, which is why we must not compare our lives to others. They have their own race with their own **Prize** created just for them, according to their design, **Purpose** and **Promise**. Paul says that everyone runs, but not everyone gets the **Prize**. For this reason, it is imperative we are not running in vain, committing to works outside of God's will. We must first make sure we are in the right race (for us) and then run to win!

> "Don't you realize that in a race everyone runs, but only one person gets the **prize**? So run to win!" (1 Corinthians 9.24 NLT).

Christ's blood covers our sins when we accept His righteousness as our own, so we won't be judged based on our repented sins when we arrive before the throne of judgment. Those have been wiped clean by the redemptive power of Christ's Blood. However, when we get to Heaven, we will be judged based on the good works we produced in obedience to the Holy Spirit. If we have sat idly on our God-given talents or if we have run a race that wasn't meant for us, we may have nothing to show for the life we led on Earth. We will receive no **Prize.** Yes, we can enter Heaven because we have been reconciled to God through Christ, but many people will have nothing to show for their years on Earth, and they may not hear the words, "Well done."

> "And I saw the dead, great and small, standing before the throne, and books were opened. Another book was opened, which is the book of life. The **dead were judged according to what they had done** as recorded in the books" (Revelation 20.12 NIV).

A great example of winning the **Prize** or Reward is found in Jesus' *"Parable of the Talents"* (Matthew 25.14-29 NKJV). In this story, there are three men to whom the Master gave Talents (money, resources, gifts, abilities, connections, etc.). To the first man, He gave five talents. To the second man, He gave two talents. And to the third man, He gave one talent. Then the Master went away, allowing His servants to steward what they had been given. The man with five talents doubled his money, and the man with two talents also doubled his money. To these two men, the Master gave them a **Prize** by making them rulers over many things, and they entered the joy of the Lord (Matthew 25.21 & 23). The third man did not multiply his talents. In fact, he just buried them away. Instead of running his race, he sat on the sidelines. This man was not given the **Prize** of rulership and joy.

The man buried his talents because he was disobedient and had the wrong view of the Master. He said the Master was a hard man without integrity (Matthew 25.24-25). Clearly, this man did not have an intimate relationship with the Master and, therefore, had a completely skewed view of Him. The Master took the one talent the third man had buried and gave it to the man who had multiplied his talents to ten. Then the third man was not allowed to experience the joy of a job well done. Finally, Jesus gave a bold statement. He said the ones who steward well will be given more, but the ones who steward poorly will be given less. Obviously, more is given to whom the Master can trust to do a good job of stewarding talents and running the race well.

> "For to **everyone who has, more will be given,** and he will have abundance; but from him **who does not have, even what he has will be taken away"** (Matthew 25.29 NKJV).

For this reason, we want to run our race to win the **Prize** of a job well done and all the rewards that it entails. Some people are scared to run their race because they will mess up and many times fail, but that is what grace is for. Grace gives us the ability to do things that scare us, that are above our pay grade and that are beyond what we ever thought we could do. Yes, we will make mistakes. Just like the person who walks more will have more opportunities to trip than the person who sits on the couch all day, but we can't let fear of mistakes prevent us from running our race.

Jesus' grace is more than enough to fill in the cracks of our imperfections. We are not called to run our race perfectly. We are called to run it with "all our heart, working as for the Lord." God, the Great Rewarder, sees our pure hearts, our honest motives, our good intentions and our hard work; and He will reward us—even if we tripped a few or even several times running our race. Remember, Jesus' Blood is constantly washing us clean (1 John 1.7 & Hebrews 9.14).

> "Whatever you do, **work at it with all your heart, as working for the Lord,** not for human masters, since you know that you will receive an inheritance from the Lord as a reward. It is the Lord Christ you are serving" (Colossians 3.23-24 NIV).

Moreover, others may give up on their race because they don't see fruit right away. In fact, they may not see fruit for years and years. However, if we are being faithful to the call of God on our lives, and we are working according to the guidance of the Holy Spirit, we must trust that we will see a **Prize** (aka a harvest) when the time is right. We can't give up hope. It is the darkest right before the dawn, which means when we think all is lost, God can instantly move His mighty hand on our behalf, watering the seeds of faithfulness we have sown all along.

If we know we are in the right race, we must trust that at the end of it will be a **Prize** if we don't give up. And once we lay hold of our **Prize**, we can be sure that our joy will overflow, and we will be so thankful that we didn't quit even when the circumstances made us believe we would never win.

> "So let's not allow ourselves to get fatigued doing good. At the right time we will **harvest a good crop if we don't give up,** or quit. Right now, therefore, every time we get the chance, let us work for the benefit of all, starting with the people closest to us in the community of faith" (Galatians 6.9-10 MSG).

The following are eight verses on God being a Rewarder of **Prizes**.

- "And behold, I am coming quickly, and My **reward** *is* with Me, to give to every one according to his work" (Revelation 22.12 NKJV).
- "I have fought the good fight, I have finished the race, and I have remained faithful. And now the prize awaits me—the crown of righteousness, which the Lord, the righteous Judge, will give me on the day of his return. And the **prize** is not just for me but for all who eagerly look forward to his appearing" (2 Timothy 4.7-8 NLT).

- "But when you pray, go into your room, close the door and pray to your Father, who is unseen. Then your Father, who sees what is done in secret, will **reward** you" (Matthew 6.6 NIV).
- "Look, I am coming soon, bringing my **reward** with me to repay all people according to their deeds" (Revelation 22.12 NLT).
- "And it is impossible to please God without faith. Anyone who wants to come to him must believe that God exists and that he **rewards** those who sincerely seek him" (Hebrews 11.6 NLT).
- "God blesses those who patiently endure testing and temptation. Afterward they will **receive the crown of life [Prize]** that God has promised to those who love him" (James 1.12 NLT).
- "Whoever welcomes a prophet as a prophet will receive a prophet's **reward**, and whoever welcomes a righteous person as a righteous person will receive a righteous person's **reward**. And if anyone gives even a cup of cold water to one of these little ones who is my disciple, truly I tell you, that

person will certainly not lose their **reward**" (Matthew 10.41-42 NIV).
- "So do not throw away this confident trust in the Lord. Remember the great **reward** it brings you!" (Hebrews 10.35 NLT).

Once we know, trust and believe that our **Place** in God encompasses **Position, Purpose, Promise, Power, Protection, Prosperity, Peace, Perfection, Provision, Prize,** we will be able to fully embrace our true identity in Christ and walk in victory every day. Then we can run our race on Earth well and be a blessing to those around us. Then when we pass from this temporal life to our eternal life with God in Heaven, we will have so much to show for our short time on Earth. We will have treasures stored up that will never fade, and our Heavenly Father will be pleased to tell us "Well done and enter into My joy."

If you enjoyed this booklet, I would love for you to leave a review on Amazon. And please check out my other award-winning fiction and non-fiction books on Amazon or my blog, www.alisahopewagner.com.

www.ingramcontent.com/pod-product-compliance
Lightning Source LLC
LaVergne TN
LVHW051155080426
835508LV00021B/2636